Sigrid Schöpe **The Handy Book of**

HORSE TRICKS

Easy Training Methods for Great Results

Includes
20
of the World's
Most Popular
Tricks!

Translated by Karen Brittle

TRAFALGAR SQUARE
North Pomfret, Vermont

First published in 2018 by
Trafalgar Square Books
North Pomfret, Vermont 05053

Originally published in the German language as
Zirkustricks mit Pferden by Franckh-Kosmos
Verlags-GmbH & Co. KG, Stuttgart

Trafalgar Square Books encourages the use of
approved safety helmets in all equestrian sports
and activities.

Library of Congress Control
Number: 2018945340

ISBN: 978-1-57076-901-6

All photos by Horst Streitferdt /Kosmos except:
pp. iii, iv, 1, 2, 3, 4, 5, 8, 9, 10 right, 22, 28, 29, 44,
45, 54, 55, 68, 69 bottom, 73, 74 by Sandra
Reitenbach / Kosmos

Book design by Atelier Krohmer, Dettingen/
Erms / English laythrough by Tim Holtz
Cover design by RM Didier
Typefaces: Capita, DIN, Frutiger, and Granjon

Printed in China

10 9 8 7 6 5 4 3 2 1

Contents

Let the Games Begin!

Playful, Fun, and Motivating

Groundwork belongs in the basic training of every horse in every discipline. It is the basis for a good partnership. If you're seeking new challenges or more variety in your training, practicing tricks with your horse can be an ideal option. Tricks are fun, increase motivation in both horse and human, and strengthen all-around confidence. Depending on which tricks you select, they can also have a suppling effect on the horse. I am sure that you and your horse will both benefit from the tricks I offer in this book.

NATURAL BEHAVIORS

The best tricks to teach are based on horses' natural behaviors. For example, a horse that wants to demonstrate dominance over another might display the Spanish Walk (see p. 26). In play-fighting, you can often see a horse rear or bow (pp. 44 and 30). It is possible to isolate these natural movements and teach the horse a specific command to execute them on cue.

Tricks are such a nice supplement to your training repertoire. Your horse will learn little tricks quite quickly. And, what's great about this is that most of the time your horse will quickly accumulate successful experiences. You'll praise your horse often and have lots of fun together, which strengthens your friendship. Allow yourself to be inspired by this book, or by attending equine expos or performances.

GOOD PREPARATION

Before beginning trick training, it is best if your horse is already familiar with basic exercises and skills learned through groundwork. These include standing quietly, allowing himself to be touched all over, and leading without a problem. And, as with any kind of schooling, you should always begin a training session with a short warm-up period to help prevent injury.

Not every trick is right for every horse. For example, with a very dominant horse, it's better not to practice rearing or Spanish Walk. In contrast, a shy horse will gain confidence through practicing work on the Pedestal. Carefully consider which exercises are right for your horse. In addition, with advanced tricks such as rearing, it's best to have a good trainer to help teach you and your horse. Every horse responds differently, and you don't want to put yourself in danger.

The Basics

In principle, you can introduce tricks to any horse regardless of age, breed, or level of training. Keep in mind your horse's character and abilities: For example, with nervous horses, it's especially important to go slowly and calmly. And while young horses often have a lot of fun learning tricks, at the same time, they may not be able to concentrate as long. When horses have health or soundness issues, you should ask your veterinarian or an experienced trainer which tricks are suitable and "do no harm."

TRUST

As I mentioned, learning tricks gives you and your horse many positive experiences. It definitely improves your relationship But, it's important you have already worked together without fear or aggression. If your horse is familiar with groundwork basics, it is easier to introduce tricks. The better his basic work, the more quickly he will understand what you want from him. This is important for keeping him motivated.

YOUR PRACTICE SPACE

Practice tricks in an enclosed area. This can be a riding ring, a round pen, or a paddock. In a grassy pasture, you probably won't find it easy to explain to your horse why he suddenly shouldn't be eating, but working instead! In the beginning, you should be alone with the horse in your practice area so that he won't be distracted. Later, after the tricks you are teaching have become routine, the presence of other horses and riders should no longer disrupt training. For some horses, it's easier when they have a friend with them in the practice space. Observe your horse to determine which environment works best for him.

For exercises that require the horse to come into contact with the ground (kneeling, lying down, bowing), softer footing is more comfortable for him.

Training Strategies

The nice thing about tricks is that later on in training, you can execute them in any order that you like and come up with interesting combinations. In this way, you'll become much freer in your practice and can do what's most fun. The horse will benefit from this approach, but only if you progress correctly in your training. It's most important that even for relatively little effort, the horse should receive lots of praise. This is motivating and contributes to making lessons a positive experience.

◄ PRAISE

Praise is the most important feedback you can give. This can consist of saying "Good!" in a happy voice, a gentle stroke on the neck, or a food treat. In the beginning, it's often wise to reward even small successes with treats, and later make your praise more verbal and only give treats now and then. After you praise the horse, allow him a short pause to think so that he can process what he's learned. Praise is so crucial to training that I will frequently remind you about it throughout this book.

IGNORE CERTAIN BEHAVIOR ▷

When the horse doesn't behave how you want him to, the best strategy is to ignore him. Perhaps he hasn't understood correctly, or doesn't yet know what he should do and has, therefore, become insecure. Repeat your signal and praise him as soon as he takes the smallest step toward the correct reaction.

TAKE YOUR TIME

Like people, horses learn very poorly when they're stressed. If you notice your horse getting nervous, the first thing to do is check in with your own state of mind. Are you calm and relaxed or have you brought the aggravations of your day with you to the horse? What signals might your body be sending without you even realizing it? How is your facial expression? Friendly? Or, is there perhaps a frown there?

Some horses get worked up when they don't understand what they're supposed to do. When this happens, go back in your training until you come to a task that your horse can do reliably. When he does it, praise him extensively. Most of the time you can resume the next day and you'll find the horse is ready for the next step. Sometimes, it simply takes longer to learn a certain trick. You should stay friendly, relaxed, and patient.

QUIT AT THE RIGHT MOMENT

With trick training, horses often cooperate with a high level of concentration and enjoy the recognition. Despite all the enthusiasm, make sure you do not overwhelm your horse by practicing too much or too long. End your training in a good moment, which will increase the horse's motivation going forward.

The Aids

The challenge when introducing exercises and tricks lies in the fact that the horse must understand your language. He recognizes what he should do based on body language and additional hand or whip signals. Therefore, it's important for you to consistently use the same signals. Commands and your body language must be so clear that it's easy for the horse to differentiate between the various tricks.

TOOLS

When used in specific ways, the halter, lead rope, and a whip or horseman's stick can help illustrate what you are asking your horse to do, as well as be part of your offering of praise when your horse tries hard to understand. It sometimes takes a bit before you can handle all these tools proficiently and so they smoothly interact. This shows how trick training also improves your coordination! With time and practice, you may be able to give up using the halter and lead rope altogether, and perform tricks at liberty.

VOICE SIGNALS

Your voice can encourage the horse, confirm his reactions, praise him, calm him down, or ask for his attention. Horses notice the inflection in our voice, so for every exercise, I use a unique vocal command to help make the trick distinguishable from others. In advanced work (and after much practice!), your horse may be able to work on voice commands alone, and know exactly what you want him to perform.

BODY LANGUAGE

Horses don't communicate with words but rather with body language. And, just as we can learn to understand the horse's body language, the horse can also learn to understand ours. Therefore, it's important that we relay clear and specific signals and become aware of how we use our body. Most of the time, we're not really aware of what our hands are doing or where we're directing our focus. For example, our shoulders and hips could open a path or block it without us even realizing.

An important element is the energy that we transmit from our body. An upright posture sends a different message to the horse than a hanging head and rounded shoulders. An energetic stride works differently than slowly moseying along. Consciously play with increasing your engagement and relaxation as you work, and observe how your horse reacts.

HAND SIGNALS

My horses respond really well to clear hand signals. Practice these with your horse! I distinguish between three especially important signals: A lifted hand means, "Stop." The horse should immediately halt and remain standing. When I rhythmically move a raised finger from left to right, I am asking my horse to yield backward. When I lift my hand, turn it toward me and give a soft, inviting wave, I'm welcoming the horse to come closer to me.

Supplies and Equipment

What materials will you need for teaching your horse the tricks in this book? This depends on what you want to do with your horse. You can work with really simple materials you already have lying around your barn or house, or you can purchase items. Ground poles, cones, barrels, and balls are all tremendously useful. If you advance to a place where you want to perform for others, you can spice up your show with colors, fabric, costumes, and other props.

BASIC EQUIPMENT

A good halter and lead rope are your most basic pieces of equipment. I like to work with a rope halter. But, it must fit well! For the lead rope, 10 to 13 feet (3 to 4 meters) is an ideal length, and I prefer to have a carabiner for the clasp. A panic snap is not necessarily good for teaching tricks as it can accidentally release the horse.

SAFETY

Regardless of whether you're working your horse on the ground or under saddle, always consider your safety and his. Practice in an enclosed area. Wear gloves because a lead rope suddenly pulled through the hands can cause injury. Sturdy shoes are equally necessary. Wear a helmet anytime you get on your horse. With Pedestal work, I recommend having boots on your horse to protect his legs.

PERFORMANCE-READY

Brightly colored props always create a good mood! Used equipment can quickly and easily be spruced up with a fresh coat of paint. Select balloons of various colors and pool noodles made of foam (most of the time they're inexpensive purchases). Ground poles and vertical pole bending poles are practical additions. A heavy tarp can be useful from time to time. Perhaps you would also like a Pedestal for specific tricks? You can purchase one from online sources, or (if you're handy) build one yourself from sturdy pallets. Cones are indispensable accessories that can be utilized in many different ways. You can purchase them cheaply at hardware or sporting goods stores. There's also so much you can do with balls of various sizes. Be creative! Note: You should be prepared for your horse initially to take a close look at any unfamiliar, brightly colored items.

TREATS

Don't ever forget to praise your horse. He will cooperate with you willingly when you spoil him a bit. I usually prefer to use small treats that the horse can chew quickly so that we can efficiently continue our practice. With Bowing (p. 30), carrots are extremely useful as they are easier to handle than a smaller treat. Note that some treats are high in sugar and may increase energy.

Warm-Up Plan

Successful artists and athletes warm up. So, as I mentioned already, before you begin practicing tricks, you should engage in a short warm-up plan. Here, too, you can get creative: Take your horse on a short walk, engage in a brief liberty or round-penning session, or longe him for a little while in both directions. In this way, his muscles will get warm and loose. Then, you can carefully begin with stretching and bending exercises.

HEAD TURN

Stand next to your horse near his neck. Place one hand on his poll and the other over his nose. Using as little pressure as possible, ask the horse to turn his head toward you. Pause briefly, slowly release, and praise the horse. After a brief pause, try the head turn on the other side. Repeat this exercise three to four times on each side.

With some horses, this exercise is easy, while others resist it. For most, it's easier on one side than the other. On this "sweet side," it's likely your horse will also allow himself to be positioned and bent more easily when ridden.

Practice carefully and in small steps. Don't force this and make sure to pay attention to your horse's signals. Practice on both sides, but begin and end on the side that is easier for him. You'll soon notice him getting suppler. Then, you can also adjust your position to be farther back along his side.

Did You Know?

Stay positive and relaxed, even if your horse doesn't understand an exercise right away. Your horse must first learn what you want from him. When you regularly incorporate bending and stretching, he will gradually be able to bring his head farther and farther back. With these exercises, you'll also notice very quickly whether your horse is holding tension. If this is the case, he will be unwilling to bend.

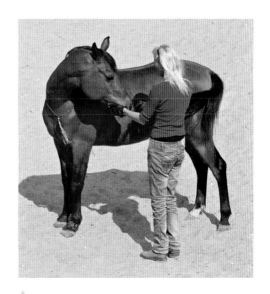

FROM HEAD TO TAIL

Position yourself next to your horse at his girth line. Place one hand on his withers, and use the other, once again, to carefully bring the horse's nose around. With horses that are willing, you can even move yourself back farther toward the horse's croup. Entice your horse with a carrot or apple.

If the horse moves easily, stand at his flank and again move his nose toward you slowly. With the other hand, grasp the end of your horse's tail. Carefully guide the horse's nose and tail together in front of your own belly. Hold this position briefly. Then slowly let go. The effect is that your horse bends along his back all the way to the base of his tail. Maintain a distance of about 1½ to 3 feet (½ to 1 meter) from the horse's flank. The farther away you stand from the horse, the more bend you require from him.

Stretching and Loosening

After tacking up, many riders lift each of the horse's front legs up and forward, holding it for a moment. The goal is to eliminate possible skin folds under the girth. With the same movement, you can loosen the horse's forehand and shoulder. The hindquarters can also be stretched somewhat before you begin working on specific tricks in your program, which can help prevent injury.

STRETCHING THE FOREHAND

Standing in front of your horse, ask him to lift the right foreleg and hold it loosely in your hand. Lift it up a bit and stretch it forward. Hold it for a moment and then carefully set it down again. Praise your horse, especially if he stands still for the stretch. Then, take the left foreleg and follow the same guidelines: lift, pull slightly forward, hold, and set down again. Practice three or four times on each side. Pay attention, making sure the horse is not lifting his head too high or getting tense through his back. My horse Shir Khan knows this exercise well and stays completely relaxed.

STRETCHING WITH A ROPE

You can also use a thick, soft rope to help stretch the horse's forehand.

Practice this stretch in an enclosed space with soft footing. To begin, test to see if the horse will allow a rope around his leg. If this works without a problem, carefully pass the rope around the front fetlock joint. Then, lightly lift the rope until the leg is stretched a bit, forward and upward. Hold this position for a brief moment and slowly set the leg down again.

It's more than enough to lift the hoof up and forward about 20 inches (50 centimeters). It's important that the horse doesn't brace against this or get thrown off balance, but stays relaxed instead. If he gets scared, immediately let go of the rozpe.

This is a good preparatory exercise for introducing the Spanish Walk later on (see p. 26).

STRETCHING THE HINDQUARTERS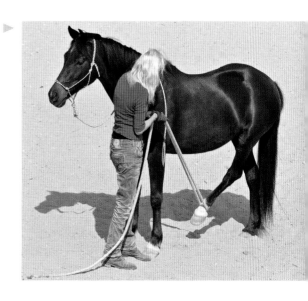

You can also stretch the hindquarters with a rope. Be especially careful when you test how the horse responds to this. Some get scared and step or jump sideways.

Slowly glide your hand over the horse's croup and hind leg (as you would when picking out his feet). Pass the rope around the fetlock joint and move it back and forth a little. Only when your horse tolerates this without any difficulty should you slowly ask him to lift the leg. The hind legs should not be lifted up as high as the front.

Slalom

Slalom through the poles can add a wonderful element to your warm-up program. Of course, you can simply lead your horse through the poles, stretching and bending him along the way. But, the exercise gets more interesting once you add in a few small surprises: for example, tie some balloons to the poles! If you don't have vertical poles (such as those used for pole bending) available, you can build a similar slalom from cones, buckets, or other items.

GOING THROUGH TOGETHER

Walk with your horse around the poles, and check to see whether he's scared of the balloons. If so, he might jump to the side when the balloons move. Be ready for this and wear both gloves and hard shoes, which you always should do for groundwork. If he can't concentrate at all with additional props, keep it simple and practice without the balloons.

SENDING YOUR HORSE THROUGH

Once you've gone through the Slalom multiple times on foot and are certain that your horse is not afraid, you can up the level of difficulty. Now, instead of going through together, ask the horse to go through alone. Stay on one side and send him on the correct path. Hold the lead rope in your left hand. Lift your right hand and point with the lead rope to show him which direction to go. To make it clearer, turn your shoulder toward the horse.

FROM A DISTANCE

Walk past one pole on the left side while your horse walks along the right side. Keep your arm stretched out for as long as you want the horse to keep a distance. Pay attention to maintaining the correct body position needed to hold him in position. Don't allow him to come toward you. In the photos, it's easy to see how attentive Duke is to the signals.

SERPENTINE

Use an inviting signal to bring the horse back onto your side. Step a bit toward the left so that the horse has room to follow you, and use your body to open up the path you desire him to follow. If you and your horse work really well together, it will also eventually become possible to do this exercise without a halter or lead rope. You'll only have to indicate to the horse where he should go.

SLALOM WITH A RIDER

You can also perform this exercise under saddle. First, ride around the poles with fairly large bends. Make sure that the horse is positioned correctly and bending around your inside leg. Look in the direction of your turn. Depending on your horse's ability, you can eventually ride tighter and tighter bends. When he responds well to leg and seat aids, try this exercise with loose reins. Once this exercise has become routine in the walk, you can also try riding the Slalom at the trot.

Free Jumping

Small jumps can also help loosen up the horse and rider. If you've already practiced groundwork on the lead rope extensively, and your horse follows you without a halter and lead (at liberty), you can try Free Jumping (in an enclosed space). Some horses have little desire to do this, while others cooperate enthusiastically.

THIS WAY

Begin your training in the arena at walk and trot. Build a small jump, ideally near the rail or fence of the ring. At first, practice with a halter and a long lead line. When your horse is following you and focused, guide him straight ahead, toward and over the jump as you walk past by his side. You go around the obstacle as your horse jumps over.

Shir Khan is well-schooled in this exercise and follows me without a halter. He pays careful attention to my signals—note he has an ear turned toward me.

FREE JUMPING

If your horse initially stops at the jump, uncertain about what to do, encourage him with your voice or touch him lightly on the flank or hindquarters with your rope. Then try again, making sure that you're directing the horse toward the jump with enough impulsion. In this scenario, it might also help if you jump over the obstacle, as well, with the horse beside you. (This way, you're improving your own fitness at the same time!)

WITH POWER

Once you've jumped over the obstacle a few times with halter and lead, and the horse has understood that he should jump beside you, try it without the halter and lead rope to see if it works. It's possible your horse will run around the jump, or he may stop and stand, unsure of what to do. In these cases, take the lead rope in one hand and use it to drive your horse on as he approaches the jump. Give your voice command, which should sound inviting and encouraging.

As with other exercises, use your imagination! For example, instead of using jump poles, change it up by jumping over a barrel lying on its side or use bales of hay.

DON'T FORGET PRAISE

Don't forget to praise, even when you're a little out of breath! This gives your horse the feedback that he has done everything well.

He'll continue to have fun with the exercise and enjoy cooperating with you. Practicing without the halter and lead rope will improve your bond.

Desensitization

Physically, your horse is now loosened up and ready for trick training, but it's also important that he's mentally stable and prepared. Build a little bit of desensitization work into your warm-up plan. Did he tend to stay relaxed with the balloons in the slalom? Then, perhaps you can try the new challenge of working with a tarp. When first faced with this exercise, many horses don't like walking over the unfamiliar, colored surface, which also makes noise.

START SLOWLY

Spread a tarp on the ground and weight it down with stones or sand so that it doesn't flap. (The tarp is already scary enough!)

Using a long lead rope, first guide your horse in a big circle around the tarp. Ignore him if he gets excited and snorts and blows as he walks beside you. If he stops and stands, quietly encourage him to walk with you. Behave as if the tarp is the most natural and normal thing in the world.

After a while, change direction so that the horse can get a good look at the tarp from both sides. Horses see the world differently with their right eye than they do with their left!

Once your horse is quieter, make your circle smaller, getting ever closer to the tarp itself. By the end of the first practice session, you should be walking over the end of the tarp as your horse walks next to you (he should not be on the tarp yet). Praise him.

Did You Know?

Always be ready for the horse to suddenly jump to the side or pull back and away from the tarp. This can happen even after you think the horse is no longer afraid. Remember: This exercise is best practiced in an enclosed space.

FIRST CONTACT

When your horse is feeling braver, go a bit closer to the tarp and let him sniff it. Perhaps you can place a few pieces of carrot or other treats on the tarp's edge. Often this is enough to convince him to touch the tarp with his nose. Some horses snort at it or try to pick it up with their teeth. Maintain a little distance so that your horse can get a good look at everything.

BRAVELY FORWARD

The next goal is for your horse to take a step onto the tarp of his own free will. If the little trick with the carrots worked, then lay the next carrot pieces a bit farther onto the tarp. In this way, you'll get the horse to step on it. Take note: With this first step, your horse can get startled by the noise and bolt away from it. Watch him closely, and if necessary, let go of the rope. Never hold on when a situation potentially becomes dangerous.

TASK COMPLETED

When you have succeeded—that is, your horse is standing on the tarp, maybe even with all four feet— praise him extensively! Approach the tarp from every direction, walking over it with your horse. If he tries to rush, stay relaxed and calm. If your horse shows fear at any point, backtrack a bit and once again circle the tarp with more or less distance.

Trick Training

After your warm-up routine, you'll be eager to begin actual work with your horse. So, let's get started with trick training. Believe it or not, I personally prefer the term "dressage at liberty" for some of these exercises! But since most of what I'm teaching would be considered "trick training" by equestrians, that's the term I will use throughout this book.

Many riders laugh at us for teaching our horses little tricks to perform. Well, what might look like useless "games" actually changes your relationship with your horse. You go beyond thinking about riding to really understanding who your horse actually is, and you learn how you can strengthen your horse's individual abilities. Many horses become more receptive and self-confident through trick training. They learn new ways of moving and improve their body awareness. You'll notice the positive effects from all this when riding.

GETTING STARTED

You don't have to train tricks in any particular order. Maybe you already have an idea of what your horse will find really fun and what will be easy for him, so you decide to begin there. Having said that, some exercises require preparation, in which case, it makes sense to introduce them step by step. For example, I always develop "Sitting" (p. 42) from "Lying Down" (p. 36). This is the logical progression based on the movement sequence of the horse, which makes it easier for him to understand what you're asking.

With all tricks, I'll try to provide the most specific directions possible. But, every horse responds differently. One will need very obvious signals; for another, a small cue is enough. Trick training helps you recognize whether your horse is more sensitive or instead needs a little more support from your aids.

OVERACHIEVER

Many horses are full of enthusiasm for the tricks they've learned and offer them even when you don't ask. When the move is new and you're pleased that the horse has offered it, you can praise him and then go directly back to the exercise or trick you are working on. Eventually, however, your horse should only perform the actual trick you're asking for. When he becomes overeager, you should ignore the behavior.

Plié

The *Plié* is an appropriate exercise to follow the warm-up as it stretches the horse's forehand, shoulders, and back. The horse lowers his head deeply and brings it between his stretched forelegs as he shifts his weight a bit toward the hindquarters. As this takes place, his neck should stay long and relaxed. This can be quite strenuous for the horse.

STARTING POINT

In the start position, the horse should stand so that his two forelegs are side by side but not too close together—he will need to be able to get his head in between them. The hind legs stand a little wider apart, in order for the horse to maintain balance. Most horses self-correct to ensure this. Take a treat and slowly bring it to the ground in front of his forelegs. Your horse will try to follow this movement. When his head comes down, allow him to eat the treat from the ground.

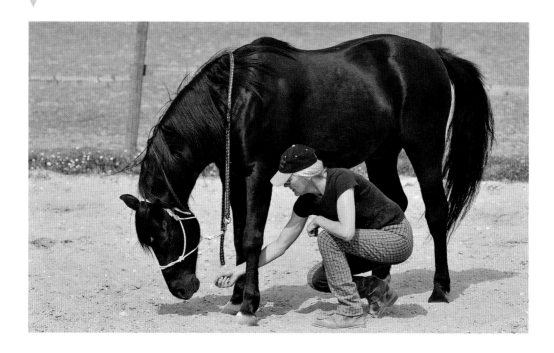

STEP BY STEP

In the second step, again take the treat down in front of his forelegs, but then quickly change hands so that you're holding it behind his front legs. Give your command ("Plié") and tap the horse lightly under his belly, at girth level. Then move your hand back a bit, allowing it to come down toward the ground as you do so. Does the horse's head follow? Make sure the horse keeps his forelegs stretched and shifts his weight backward. If it doesn't work, start over. Often this exercise works best with a carrot as the horse can see it.

DEEP BOW

It's uncomfortable for many horses to keep their legs stretched out in front. They try to avoid the stretch and bend their joints. To avoid this issue, end the exercise just before it happens. Reward the horse, allow him to exit the position, and start again from the beginning. With each try, you should attempt to bring your hand a little farther back, without having the horse bend the fetlock joints. When the exercise is done correctly, your horse will have his forelegs stretched before him and his head between his legs, with his forehead on or almost on the ground. The horse should only hold this position for a short time (it's strenuous).

Spanish Walk

The *Spanish Walk* looks impressive and can be learned by almost every horse, at least in hand. Later, talented horses are also able to demonstrate this movement under saddle. Alternating sides, the horse lifts his forelegs almost to a horizontal level and moves forward as he does so. A prerequisite for this exercise is that the horse is already used to being touched with the rope, stick, or whip.

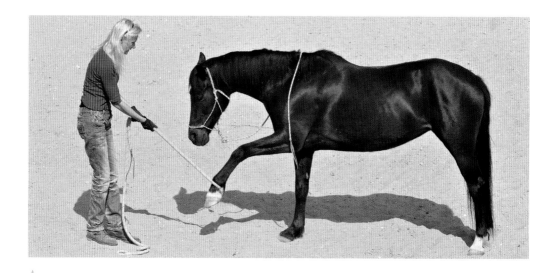

LIFTING THE LEG

For this step of teaching the trick, stand in front of the horse and carefully place a long, soft rope around one front fetlock joint. Lightly lift the leg and hold it in this position for a moment, then set it slowly down again. Praise him! Next, take the rope in one hand and a whip in the other. Touch your horse's shoulder with the whip and give the command (for example, "Paso," which is "Step" in Spanish). Repeat the exercise on both sides. It can be a little easier if you have a friend to help by taking over handling the rope.

It won't take long to get to the point where you will no longer need the rope. You will stand near the horse, and he will lift his leg based on the whip and voice command. As time goes by, the horse will lift his leg higher and stretch it farther.

POLKA

Most horses find it difficult to execute the Spanish Walk while moving forward. Most move only their forelegs while their hindquarters practically stand still. The horse's body gets progressively longer, and he eventually loses his balance.

In order to get forward movement combined with the Spanish Walk, you can use a trick: *The Polka*. Stand with your horse on the track along the rail of the arena (so that he has some support from the fence line or wall) and first touch the inside shoulder (the one to the inside of the arena) and say "Paso"; let your horse take two normal steps, then tap his *outside* shoulder and say again, "Paso"; follow this with two normal steps, and so on. With this three-part rhythm, the hind legs will also step up nicely at the same time, and the movement sequence becomes fluid. The horse's head and neck position should stay as relaxed as possible.

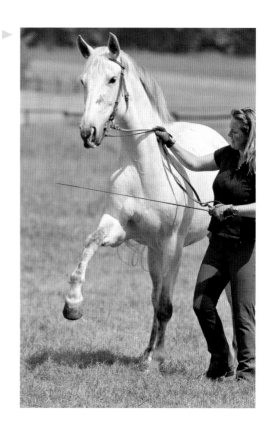

ALTERNATING SIDES

More and more frequently, allow the horse to "miss a step," until your horse is actually lifting his leg high in Spanish Walk, but alternating from side to side. Carry yourself upright and maintain your position at the horse's shoulder.

Be careful not to overwork your horse. You should always give him one or two rounds of the arena in a totally normal walk. Quit this exercise before your horse is tired and before his strides have become less expressive. Throughout, pay attention to whether he is lifting through his back.

Spanish Walk with a Rider

A horse demonstrating Spanish Walk under saddle is a truly beautiful sight. The transition to doing this exercise under saddle will be easier for both horse and rider if you have a helper who can give the familiar signal from the ground. Begin with the Polka (see p. 27), as it's easier for the horse to transition this way. If your horse has already mastered the Spanish Walk on the ground, he will likely learn it quickly with a rider.

SITTING CORRECTLY

At first, practice the Spanish Walk with your horse under saddle while standing still. From the saddle, touch his inside shoulder and give your command. At the same time, your helper on the ground should also give the familiar hand signal. Shift your weight to the other side of the saddle—so, if the horse is lifting his left leg, you shift your weight to the right and vice versa. Take note: Do not fold at your hips when you shift your weight.

THE AIDS

To ask the horse to lift his left leg, you should give the following aids: Bring your left leg slightly away from the horse's side. Shift your weight to the right side. Lightly lift your left hand/rein. Make sure that the horse stays straight in his neck and remember to release the rein. You'll know that the horse has become crooked if you see that his ears are no longer at the same height. When this occurs, the best thing to do is start over. For the right leg, the same aids apply but on the opposite side.

At first, just practice asking the horse to lift his legs at the halt—do not ask for the whole movement sequence. Make sure that you are regularly changing the side you're practicing on.

FLUIDLY FORWARD

If everything is working well at a standstill, you can try the Polka in the saddle while moving forward. Make sure that your aids are soft and not jerky. A touch of the whip to the shoulder supports your aids. You should stay upright in the saddle and resist the urge to lean over and try to see how high the horse is lifting his legs. You can still give your voice command in rhythm from the saddle.

Make sure you do not underestimate how much physical effort it means for your horse. Quit before your horse becomes tired and unwilling. One long side of the riding arena is more than enough. With further training, the horse can demonstrate more steps.

The Bow

The Bow is one of the most popular tricks. However, some horses find it difficult in the beginning—they feel more secure when they're standing on all four feet. Please don't force it. To complete this exercise, the horse must balance on three legs, which cultivates trust. If you're new to trick training, please enlist the help of a trainer experienced in this kind of exercise to show you what you need to pay attention to in order to ensure success.

◀ HOLDING THE LEG UP

Always be especially careful when practicing The Bow. It has many positive effects, but also increases the risk for injury. Therefore, it's important to warm up your horse. Make sure you're working on footing that is soft and comfortable. Does your horse have back problems? In this case, The Bow is probably not the right trick to work on—choose something else.

Position yourself at the girth line, with your gaze directed toward the horse's head. Taking this position distinguishes The Bow from your daily request to "pick up" a hoof. A clear voice command will also help your horse differentiate between the two.

Practice having the horse pick the leg up and holding it for a few seconds. Then, have him set the leg down again and praise your horse. Some horses will lift their leg when signaled to do so with the whip; with others, you'll have to take the leg in your hand.

Don't work with force. If need be start over and try again. When your horse stays quiet, continue.

BALANCE

Lift the horse's leg again and have him hold in this position long enough so that he can find his balance. Next, walk a step backward so the lifted leg moves slightly backward, then slowly allow the horse to set the leg down and ask him to stand up square.

If your horse doesn't understand what you want from him when it comes to The Bow, it often helps to show him the way down with his head and body, using a carrot or other treat. But, make sure that he doesn't only concentrate on the treat and gobble it up quickly. He should move downward slowly and with control so that he doesn't hurt himself or you.

Did You Know?

You can often observe horses bow when they are playing with one another. It is a natural horse behavior, which people can train the horse to do on command.

SWAYING

When first training this more challenging version of the trick, you should praise your horse for even a gentle sway backward, even if he doesn't get to the point of actually lowering a foreleg to the ground. Calmly try again until your horse finally trusts enough to lower his leg. You can also lightly press against his chest with your hand and in this way gently push him backward, encouraging the movement you wish for. In time, it will be enough to give your horse the voice command and touch his cannon bone with your whip. Once the horse understands what you want from him, pay close attention to make sure he's doing the exercise correctly. The leg that's in front should remain outstretched. In the picture below, my horse Romeo could lift his back up more.

Work on getting your horse to hold The Bow. He'll be likely to do so if you provide him with food on the ground.

The Bow with a Rider

Once your horse has mastered The Bow correctly and confidently, you can progress to the next step: to execute the trick under sadde. It's again a good idea to have a helper on the ground in the beginning. The helper can give the horse the signal from the ground, which he has now come to trust. Practice in an arena or enclosed space with footing the horse finds comfortable, and pay careful attention to whether your horse seems uncomfortable at any point.

TWO PEOPLE TO PRACTICE

Ask your helper to stand near your horse. As the rider, you can tap the horse's leg with the whip (giving the signal to Bow) and give the voice command, or you can ask your helper to take over and do so, which allows you to concentrate on your horse and your seat.

On the first try, it's best for you to sit completely passively and lean back just slightly. Maintain a light contact on the reins. As training progresses, you become more active and the helper is then only there for support.

Did You Know?

If you incorporate a tap from the whip to the horse's leg when training The Bow from the ground, you'll have it easier later when attempting to train this exercise under saddle. Your horse will recognize the command and know what it means.

Note: It's best to have your horse wear protective boots or polo wraps when training The Bow, so his legs are protected.

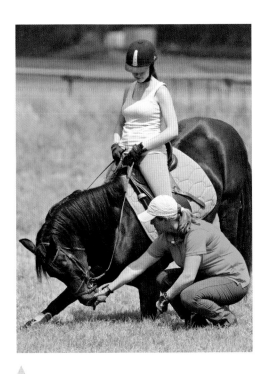

If you've practiced this exercise carefully and calmly, your helper will soon become unnecessary. You'll tap your horse's fetlock joint with the whip (always with the voice command, for example, "Bow"). Allow your hands to come forward a bit and shift your weight back lightly so that you don't fall onto the horse's shoulders. Make sure that your horse's neck stays straight and he's not sagging through his back.

When your horse is bowing, leave the whip in front of the leg for a moment and give the command for him to stand up. Be prepared—your horse might jump back up into a square position.

Praise your horse for this fantastic effort!

WELL DONE!

As long as your horse remains in The Bow, you or your helper should hold the whip in front of his kneeling leg for a few seconds. This signals to the horse that he should stay down. Ideally, the helper should directly praise the horse from the ground. Then, with a clear signal, allow the horse to stand back up and praise him again. As the rider, you should try to stay in balance as he stands up. An unbalanced rider can make the horse insecure.

In the beginning, it may be that the horse cannot maintain a Bow for very long with a rider. Build this up slowly. Be satisfied with just a little bit!

Kneeling

Kneeling is most often developed from The Bow. Here, too, there are various approaches to training the trick. I'm going to present you with a method that has been successful for me. Because horses bend their forelegs when they lie down, they are familiar with the sequence of movements that leads to Kneeling and typically prefer it to lowering into a Bow. Under no circumstances should the head come between the knees as it would in Plié (see p. 24), but instead it should stay straight or turn to the side.

◀ A REFLEX

Does your horse automatically bow when you tap his leg? Take advantage of this! At just the moment in which the horse is bending his leg and wants to lay it down, tap the other leg with the whip (the one that would normally stay stretched out in a bow).

Don't expect that your horse will instantly understand what you are so surprisingly now asking from him. If he simply bows again, ask him to stand up and start over. You must find the right moment to tap the leg on the other side.

Make sure that you're standing next to your horse—not in front of him. Use a clear voice command, such as "Kneel." With any luck, your horse will eventually actually bend both legs at the knee. Praise him effusively at precisely that moment! This way he'll know he's on the right track.

As with all tricks, you can enlist the support of an experienced trainer here or observe a clinic in order to gather valuable tips and information. As an observer, you can also watch the horses carefully and see how the trainer approaches your horse's personality.

UNDERSTANDING THE SIGNAL

Encourage your horse as soon as he's on the right track. The closer he comes to Kneeling, the more you praise him. If he kneels, pause a moment, and then allow him to stand up with the familiar voice command.

Repetition leads to success. Try it again and again. Soon your horse will know: When the second leg is also tapped, you're asking him to Kneel!

CONFIRMING THE EXERCISE

With good preparation and sensitive horses, this method works. In the beginning, I advise having a helper on the opposite side who can support the horse in bringing his second leg back.

Heads up: Your horse may jump up out of The Bow because he doesn't exactly know what you want from him and is unsure in this position. Stay calm! Try it again: Tap the leg, and before he stretches his other leg out, you (or your helper) should tap the opposite leg, too.

Lying Down

From a Kneeling position, it's relatively easy for the horse to learn *Lying Down*. Still, this trick is asking a lot of the horse, as to lie down on command is a huge vote of confidence coming from a flight animal. Only a few horses will deliberately lie down directly near their rider. The movement sequence itself is not complicated. Practice when your horse is relaxed and not just before feeding time. Select a quiet, familiar place to school, and be patient when it doesn't work right away.

STARTING POINT

Allow your horse to Kneel. Use the lead rope like a rein and turn the horse's head toward the side opposite from where you are standing. Make sure that you are clearly standing to the side, in line with his shoulder. Now take the lead rope a bit toward you, so that the horse takes his head sideways and back toward his tail. If you're lucky, the horse will give into the movement and allow himself to tip to the side.

SPACE TO LIE DOWN

With some horses, Lying Down works right away, but others will require more patience. Give it time. Be careful: Make sure you're not standing too close to the horse so that he has enough room. Praise your horse immediately! Perhaps he'll jump right back up again, in which case, you should still praise him. When he jumps up, the horse will stretch out his forelegs. Therefore, it's important that you're never standing in front of your horse.

SHORT TRAINING SESSIONS

Always work on this trick in short sessions and incorporate your voice command (for example "Down" or "Lie Down"), ideally with a hand signal also.

In the photos, you can recognize that Romeo is Lying Down based only on my hand signal. You can also incorporate a signal from the whip so that later under saddle, your horse will associate this exercise with a touch of the whip in a certain place (for example, on the cannon bone). He'll immediately know that he should lie down.

Did You Know?

Many horses have a tendency to roll when they Lie Down. Try to prevent this! This puts you in great danger, regardless of whether you're working from the ground or under saddle. As soon as your horse gives the smallest indication that he's going to roll, you must immediately "shoo" him to his feet. He must not be allowed to associate the Lie Down with rolling; rather, these must remain clearly separate.

Lying Down with a Rider

As soon as your horse has understood that he should Lie Down based on a hand signal and touch from the whip, and that he should stay Lying Down for a bit, you can try Lying Down under saddle. Once again, I recommend working with a helper. Here, if your horse gets a familiar signal from the ground, he will more quickly understand what he's supposed to do. Make sure that he does not become excited or frantic.

DOWN WE GO

If your horse understands the signal, he will bend his forelegs. Move your upper body back a bit and give him a free rein. Now your horse will come down to his knees to Lie Down. Stay loose and relaxed, even when it feels really strange. As soon as your horse lies down, praise him and immediately get off, as he's likely to immediately jump back up again. If he's so good as to stay down, you can calmly give him the voice command to stand back up.

FEET OUT

Take your feet out of the stirrups for this exercise, so that you can immediately dismount when your horse lies down. Make sure you're wearing sturdy shoes that won't become caught in the stirrups. The reins should lie loosely over the horse's neck. You or your helper should tap the horse's cannon bone with the whip (as you practiced on the ground) and give the familiar voice command.

STANDING UP

Gradually increase the amount of time the horse should remain Lying Down. If that's going well, you're ready to try the next step: you stay in the saddle, give the command to stand up—and your horse stands up again *with you still in the saddle*. But, please, don't try everything at once! You should only increase the difficulty once the Lie Down with the rider is going well.

If your horse jumps up from the Lie Down, grab mane and remain relaxed in the saddle. Praise your horse before you dismount.

Taking a Nap

Is your horse now well-practiced at Lying Down? Will he stay down for a longer time with you on the ground, without becoming restless? Then, it's time for a new challenge: *Taking a Nap* is a very popular trick and can (in various ways) become the successful end to a public performance. Or, it can make for a funny beginning (when your horse must first "wake up" to do the show).

TRY IT OUT

Sit down near your horse when he's Lying Down and attempt to slowly and carefully bring your horse's head down until it's lying on the ground. This is new and unfamiliar. Be ready for your horse to jump up. Pay attention to your position and don't force him. This exercise requires time and trust—no pressure!

STAYING DOWN

If your horse stays with you on the ground and lays his head down, you can stroke his neck and praise him with a quiet voice. If he'll eat, you can give him a treat.

As always, this takes practice and patience. If you've already instilled your horse with lots of trust when practicing Lying Down, this exercise will work, too.

A VOTE OF CONFIDENCE

If your horse tries to stand up, allow him to do so. It's likely that you'll cause him to panic if you hold him down, and this puts you in danger. Force is not necessary and it's also totally useless—a horse that's stressed will not Lie Down. Always try again with patience. With time, the horse will be more secure, then he'll also stay Lying Down for a longer time.

Make sure that you are sitting behind your horse and that he doesn't want to roll. If your horse lies calmly on his side, stroke him. Keep a good eye on him. If he stays calm and relaxed while Lying Down,

you can also try to place your head on the horse's shoulder. To do this, you need a lot of trust in your horse, and him in you. Enjoy the deep connection.

Did You Know?

Taking a Nap is an extreme vote of confidence on the part of the horse. You should really treasure it. In order to recognize whether your horse is relaxed, watch his legs as he's Lying Down: if they are lying loose and quietly on the ground, your horse feels good.

Sitting

It's easiest for the horse to learn to do *Sitting* out of Lying Down. When it's possible for you to control his standing up, step by step, it's essentially already learned. To get to this point, the horse must already have really mastered Lying Down and also be willing to remain Lying Down without jumping up again immediately of his own accord.

STOPPING THE MOVEMENT

When your horse wants to get up after Lying Down, he'll stretch his forelegs out in front of him. At this moment, stop your horse here with a treat. Or, give an active command (for example, "Sit") with the signal to do so, holding a treat in your hand. The horse will lift his head in order to get the treat. As soon as he's stretched his legs—but only if he stays on the ground—give the treat and praise him.

GETTING HIGHER

In the next step, your horse should straighten his forelegs. You can again work with a reward. I'm standing in front of Romeo here, as he's already mastered this exercise. In the beginning, you should stand to the side of your horse and give the voice command "Sit," along with a hand signal. Hold your hand with the reward over the horse's head. Your horse must come up higher in order to get the treat.

SMALL STEPS

Praise your horse as soon as he has come up a little higher with his forelegs, right at the moment before he wants to jump up to a standing position. On the next attempt, you can try to get your horse to come up a little higher. Don't expect your horse to Sit immediately, but rather work step by step to get a little higher.

As soon as your horse has understood the hand signal and voice command, stand on the side of your horse when he's Lying Down, say "Sit," give him the hand signal (with the hand in which you're holding the treat), and wait for your horse to slowly sit up. Praise every good response. You'll get the individual phases of rising under control and your horse will not have the impulse to immediately jump to his feet. By and by, reduce the reward and only praise him when the trick is completed.

Rearing Up in Hand

As a young horse, Romeo had already learned to rear through play. There are, however, other methods for training a horse to *Rear*. I can't describe all the methods in this book, so I'll select the method that is easiest to follow. But first, once again, an important tip: Not every horse is meant to learn this exercise. Before attempting it, you should absolutely have a clear understanding of "Who's the boss?" in your relationship. I never train very dominant horses to rear.

◀ AN INTERESTING GAME

Work with a halter and a long lead rope of 10 to 13 feet (3 to 4 meters). Stand in front of your horse and try to "initiate play," by shaking the lead rope a bit and then suddenly taking a step toward your horse. Make sure you always leave enough distance for safety. At first, your horse won't understand what you want from him. Try out this playful scenario again and again. If your horse comes toward you, then send him back to his position. He should never stand close enough to you that he could hurt you.

Closely observe your horse's reaction, paying attention to his facial expression and body language. If he appears nervous or annoyed, stop. Consider again whether your horse is suited to be trained to Rear on command.

UP

It's likely that your horse, at first, will be trying to figure out what exactly you want from him. In the beginning, it can happen that he simply tosses his head up high. Even then, you should immediately praise him.

Try it once again. Lift your arms up high and calmly give the voice command, for example, "Up!" Maybe your horse lifts his forelegs from the ground (most likely by coincidence). That's just great, so praise him!

Most horses will now quickly learn what they're supposed to do. After a short time, your horse will bring the forehand higher and higher. In the beginning, you should practice regularly, every two to three days, for about 10 minutes, and always following the same routine. Don't forget your voice command. Every positive reaction is praised immediately.

SAFETY FACTORS

Correct Rearing depends, above all, on your clear body language. Make yourself large and dominant, but always keep paying attention to your safe distance from your horse. I've trained Romeo to know that he must first take two to three steps backward in this exercise before I'll give him the command to Rear. In this way, he maintains a good distance from me.

Only once your horse can securely Rear *on* the lead rope, and *only* when you command him to do so, can you try it *off* the lead rope.

Rearing with a Rider

You say you want your horse to Rear under saddle? This requires a little courage, and you should only consider this when Rearing on the ground is going well with hand signals and a verbal command. At first, you'll practice just as you did without a rider, which means a helper takes over your position on the ground. The helper stands a distance from the horse, gives the familiar voice command to Rear, and also uses the relevant body language.

THE RIDER'S POSITION

When Rearing with a rider, it's important you "give" on the reins and sit up straight. Allow your legs to be a bit farther back and bend forward slightly at the waist as soon as the horse rears up.

Don't get scared when the horse's neck comes toward you. Position your head slightly to one side. Once you and your horse have established a routine, you can reduce the degree to which you bend forward.

WELL DONE

When the horse is Rearing willingly on command (and *only* on command), he should be praised extensively. Under no circumstance should you praise the horse if he demonstrates this little trick without being told to do so. You must definitely prevent him from Rearing on his own accord; otherwise, it becomes dangerous. In this case, you had better stop practicing this exercise.

If Rearing with a rider is working well and happening calmly, you can practice without a helper. Begin at the center of the arena and give the familiar command. Does your horse Rear? If not, ask your helper to support you once again.

A CLEAR SIGNAL

In order to avoid having Romeo associate Rearing under a rider with moving backward (which would likely cause him to want to Rear whenever he's asked to back up, as the rider's position is similar in both cases), I have built in an additional signal when I ask my horse to Rear under saddle: I pull a bit on a piece of his mane at the same moment I give the command to Rear.

If you and your horse have enough routine and confidence, you can increase the artistry even further by trying the Rear while you're riding bareback. You can also integrate it into a performance, if that is something you aspire to do with your horse.

The Pedestal

To perform *The Pedestal* trick, handy people can build themselves a Pedestal fairly easily. You just need one or two wooden pallets, a plywood board the same size as the pallets, and/or a thick rubber mat for the top surface. Note: A Pedestal made from two pallets is very heavy! Screw the pallets together and nail the mat or plywood on top. Beneath the artificial turf, you must always nail down the pallets, or else the Pedestal won't be stable enough.

GETTING USED TO IT

Lead your horse toward the Pedestal. Let him sniff it all over. Stand on the Pedestal yourself, to show your horse that this wooden thing is completely harmless. If your horse stands quietly near the Pedestal, praise him.

Stand your horse in front of the Pedestal, and try to get him to touch the Pedestal with his hoof. If it doesn't work, perhaps a helper can lift the horse's foreleg and set the hoof on the Pedestal, holding it there briefly.

MORE ADVANCED

Entice your horse forward until he sets the second hoof on the Pedestal. Praise, praise, praise! Don't immediately try asking your horse to get all four feet on the Pedestal, and definitely do not try if you have a horse that is cautious or unsure. Allow your horse to stand briefly on the Pedestal.

Attention: Even calm and quiet horses can jump suddenly off the Pedestal out of fear. Never stand in front of your horse but always a bit off to the side until your horse is confident with this trick.

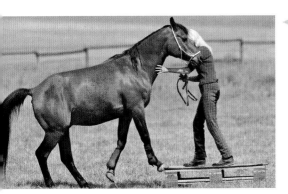

BACKWARD

Guide your horse backward off the Pedestal. He should not walk forward across it yet. Make sure that he doesn't step on himself or slip off the side. If you have a very calm and motivated horse that is offering of his own accord to climb onto the Pedestal with all four feet, you can, of course, allow him to do so.

Exercises on the Pedestal

As soon as your horse will easily step onto the Pedestal with his front legs, you can try to get him to stand up there with all four feet. Here, too, it can be useful to have a helper in the beginning. If your horse is relaxed and easy to work with, you can try it on your own. Remember that you should never stand directly in front of your horse in case he decides to bolt forward suddenly.

FOUR HOOVES ON THE PEDESTAL

Slowly entice your horse onto the Pedestal. As soon as your horse has all four feet up, praise him and allow him to stand there totally relaxed for a while. If your horse doesn't trust himself to step onto the Pedestal, a helper can encourage him from behind with the light touch of a whip. But be careful: Don't create too much pressure! The horse should step up with control.

CLIMBING DOWN

This time, lead your horse forward off the Pedestal, one step at a time. Once all four hooves are on the Pedestal, this is much easier than stepping backward to get down. In addition, doing so would greatly increase the chances of your horse injuring himself.

TURNING ON THE PEDESTAL

Over time, you can build in variations to keep your work on the Pedestal interesting.

One new task, for example, is to turn while on the Pedestal. This is truly a difficult exercise, during which many horses try to step off the Pedestal on one side.

In the beginning, simply try to get the horse to move a little on the Pedestal. Many horses require lots of convincing to do so; many lack the confidence. A half or quarter turn is enough at first. Allow the horse to stand quietly and process, praise him and then practice further. If the horse tries to get down, guide him (forward) off the Pedestal altogether and start over from the beginning.

Always pay attention to the position of the horse's hooves. If your horse is getting close to the edge of the Pedestal, correct him and get him back in the middle.

SPANISH WALK

If your horse enjoys work on the Pedestal, you can see whether he'll perform a Spanish Walk on it. Have him stand with two, or four, feet on the Pedestal, point to a shoulder and give the command that he learned in your earlier work (see p. 26). Or pick up a front leg, hold it for a moment, then place it down again.

Pedestal Work with a Rider

Many horses have a lot of fun with Pedestal work. Don't practice every day as that's too much for the horse and he may lose his motivation to perform. If your horse will step onto the Pedestal with all four feet without a problem, you can also try it from your horse's back—under saddle. In this way, you can build this exercise into your under-saddle training to provide variety.

WITH A HELPER

For safety, you should first allow yourself to be led onto the Pedestal. This gives you and your horse more security in the beginning and the trick will be clearer for him. As soon as your horse stands on the Pedestal, he should be praised by both you and your helper. To conclude this trick, your helper should guide the horse backward off the Pedestal.

Only once this is all working well with the rider and the helper, and your horse is staying calm, should you try it alone from the saddle.

REWARD

Many horses feel suddenly insecure when they get on the Pedestal with a rider on their back. Patience, a calm approach, and treats help him get over these initial difficulties quite quickly—most of the time. Don't force the horse, but rather practice a few more times in hand if he doesn't want to step onto the Pedestal with a rider. Romeo is well practiced and at ease performing this trick, so we can even do this bareback.

WITH PURPOSE

When you're ready to try without a helper, ride onto the Pedestal. If your horse will stand on the Pedestal with his front legs, stay there for a moment, praise him, then take an easy step backward to get down again.

If your horse tries to avoid by stepping to the side, you can perhaps position the Pedestal alongside a fence or ask a helper to remain standing next to the Pedestal.

A PROUD PAIR

It won't take long for you and your horse to get used to stepping onto the Pedestal. Soon, the horse will also do so with all four feet. Many horses love the Pedestal because they are elevated while on it— lifted above everything and able to see all around them. They prefer an elevated position in the wild where flight animals have a better view of the world. This trick is a very good idea for those horses that may need an increase in self-confidence.

Brain Training for Your Horse

Tricks are brain training for your horse. They actually make your horse more clever and capable when he has to figure out new tasks. Tricks offer you the opportunity to take your horse's preferences into consideration. If you're able to inspire your horse's enthusiasm during training, it is of benefit to you both. And if you choose to perform in public, you'll certainly enjoy your audience's look of amazement: tricks allow you to put together a wonderful little show of all you and your horse have accomplished together. In this book I am introducing you to my favorite tricks, which my horses also have fun with. Again, carefully consider what you want to teach your horse—even "little" tricks can sometimes have their drawbacks.

EYE CONTACT

In contrast to riding, you can observe your horse much more easily during groundwork. Is he tense and restlessly swishing his tail? Does he look interested or does he seem unsure? Is he concentrating on the task at hand or allowing himself to be easily distracted?

Pay attention to your horse's facial expression: Does he understand what you want from him? Is he having fun? Is he finding the exercise challenging or is it easy for him?

You can use trick training to help you "listen" more closely to your horse and really understand him better. This improves your connection in everything you do together.

POSSIBLE "SIDE EFFECTS"

I trained Romeo to take off his blanket. Many people have said to me, "Yeah...but if he knows how to take a blanket off for a trick, then he's going to take off ALL his blankets! I don't want that!" It is a fair question, as do any of us want our horses taking off their expensive turnout blankets, possibly tearing them as they do so?

This doesn't have to be the case. But, you should get the training of this trick right from the beginning. From the start, you must give clear signals and ignore your horse if he demonstrates tricks you haven't asked for. Ask yourself if you inadvertently gave a signal and didn't realize it. The area where you practice is another deciding factor. Never practice this trick in the stall or stable aisle, but in a neutral location.

Taking My Blanket Off

Taking My Blanket Off is a wonderful trick, but in order to avoid your horse removing every blanket that he wears, you should only use a specific, completely ordinary blanket when requesting this trick. Do not do it with a cooler or turnout blanket, but just an inexpensive blanket from a department store. As mentioned, make sure to only practice in a specific place, such as your riding arena. In this way, you avoid having your horse get the idea that he can remove his blanket in the barn aisle, paddock, or stall, as you won't attempt this trick in these locations under any circumstance.

BASIC PRINCIPLE

Head to the riding arena with your horse, the blanket, and a few treats (I like to use apple pieces). Now, place the blanket loosely over your horse's back, take hold of one front corner, lift it lightly and say, "Hold" or "Take." The goal is for your horse to turn his head toward you, take the corner of the blanket in his mouth and turn his head back to the front again. As he does so, he'll automatically pull the blanket from his back.

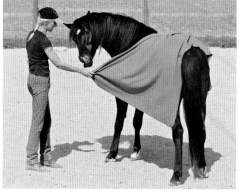

APPLE TRICK

At first, it's likely that your horse won't show much interest in the blanket. This is where the apple comes into play: Use an apple piece to rub the corner of the blanket that you want the horse to take in his mouth. As soon as your horse grasps onto the corner of the blanket, praise him and give him the apple or a treat. When you're just starting out, you want to reward the horse just for mouthing or lipping the corner of the blanket.

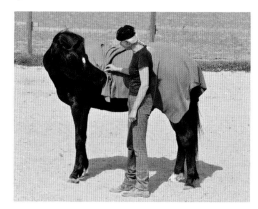

IT JUST HAPPENS

Once your horse will take the blanket in his mouth, removing his blanket will follow almost all by itself. His head will move, either back to the front or up or down. If you're lucky, the blanket will stay in his mouth as this takes place, and so he almost coincidentally removes the blanket from his back. If it doesn't happen, just try again. Praise your horse immediately! Horses learn very quickly what you want from them.

If this trick is working well, you can practice with your horse so that he "hands you" the blanket: As soon as he removes the blanket, hold your hand out quickly and catch the blanket as it falls out of his mouth. Praise again. You can also "trade" the blanket for a small treat. If the horse immediately lets the blanket fall, don't praise him.

Over time, you'll get to the point where your horse waits for you to take the blanket out of his mouth.

Taking Your Hat Off

Taking Your Hat Off is a trick well suited for a quieter horse. However, when you have a horse that tends to like to grab at things, you want to avoid this trick. The danger is that the horse will grasp the hat too roughly and hurt you as he does so. Carefully consider whether this exercise belongs in your repertoire.

GENTLE ENOUGH?

Position yourself in front of your horse and rub the brim of an old ball hat with a piece of apple, for example. In the beginning, hold the hat a bit above your head, instead of really setting it on your head. This way you can test whether your horse is going to grasp it gently enough.

If your horse will playfully take the hat in his mouth, immediately build a voice command into the exercise sequence.

VERY CAREFULLY

Once you get the sense that your horse is being careful enough to safely perform the trick, take the next step: Set the hat on your head and try asking your horse to "Take it off." As you do so, go down on one knee. Use your hand to indicate the brim of the hat and give your voice command. Can you see how carefully my horse Romeo is taking my hat in his mouth? I drop my head a little so that the hat practically slides off by itself.

GIVE IT BACK

Your horse will likely advance quickly, and you can make the trick more challenging so that he doesn't get bored: After your horse removes your hat, he should now give it back to you.

If your horse drops the hat immediately, praise him but do not give him a treat. If your horse holds onto it for a short time longer so you have the time to take it out of his mouth, he should be rewarded with a treat.

GOOD!

Learning tricks primarily happens through praise. You must always find the right moment to give your horse positive feedback. This can't be too soon, but also can't be too late.

Here, you need exact timing and an instinct about your horse's reactions. This is your personal challenge with this trick.

Crossing the Legs

Crossing the Legs is a trick that has a lot of audience appeal. It almost looks as if the horse is saying, "I'll go this far, but not a step past that!" or "No, I don't like that." This makes it easy to incorporate this trick into your little show when you perform in public...maybe you cross your own legs along with your horse, which looks really funny!

STAY RELAXED

To teach your horse to cross his legs, you should stand near your horse's shoulder. Now, take the near foreleg in your hand and move it gently back and forth. In this way, you can see if your horse allows you to move his leg in a loose and relaxed manner.

SHIFT YOUR WEIGHT

Sometimes the horse may be insecure and will not eagerly lift his leg up. In this case, lean a bit against your horse's shoulder. Then, he'll probably shift his weight more onto the standing leg and you can lift and move the leg on your side.

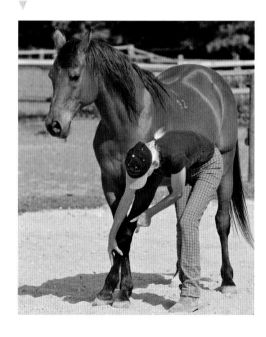

MOVING IT OVER

Guide the lifted leg lightly over the other and hold it there for a moment. Remember to build in a vocal command, for example, "Cross." Afterward, move the leg back slowly.

As a next step, cross the leg over the opposite front leg, hold it in this position and say, for example, "Stay," so that your horse learns to hold the leg there. As you bring the leg back, you can give another command, "Done." After several attempts, cross the leg over and say, "Stay," then take your hand away. If your horse keeps the leg there (even for just a short time), praise him. Most horses will want to "reorganize" their legs as quickly as possible. If your horse stays in this position, he trusts you. Remain patient.

Once you feel that your horse understands what he should do, cross his leg over with your foot instead of your hand: Lay your hand on his neck or withers, say, "Cross," and use your foot to push the horse's leg over. If your horse crosses his legs, follow up with the command, "Stay," and after a second say, "Done." Later, you'll be able to just tap quickly on your horse's hoof and use your voice commands for him to perform the trick.

You can increase the challenge by crossing your legs alongside your horse so that he crosses his legs at the same time you do—synchronized!

Not every horse is meant to perform this trick. He should be on the quieter and more relaxed side. Also, at first, as with Taking Off the Blanket, you should only practice in a designated place.

Tug of War

Tug of War is a fun little trick. You need only a length of rope—an old lead rope (with metal hooks and clasps removed) works perfectly. This exercise is a good one for curious horses that like to put everything in their mouth. Begin with a short rope; later you can try using a longer one. You will be asking your horse to learn to hold on to something and not let go. And that means one thing: practice, practice, practice!

OFFER

Take the end of the rope and rub it with apple (or another treat that your horse likes) in order to make the end of the rope "appetizing." Hold this end of the rope toward your horse. As soon as the horse takes the rope into his mouth, praise him. Practice this until your horse immediately takes the rope into his mouth, as soon as you hold it in his direction.

HOLD

Next, see if you can persuade the horse to keep the rope in his mouth a little longer. This is a matter of practice and, of course, develops over time. Have patience! The rope should be thick so that if your horse chews he doesn't work his way loose and doesn't rip it when he tries to pull—which is the next step.

PULL IT

At first, try just lightly pulling the rope—with only a little strength and under no circumstance jerking on it. Praise your horse if he keeps the rope in his mouth. (But make sure you don't praise him at the moment that he lets go!) If he won't hold on to the rope, refrain from praising him, and just start over again.

It will take some time before your horse understands what you want from him in this trick.

THE CONTEST

Now (and only now!), you can really pull on the rope as you would if you were playing tug of war. Do not jerk, but instead pull slowly and steadily, until you're able to hang on to the rope, using your whole body weight. But heads up: Your horse is likely to let go quite suddenly! Only practice this trick in an area with soft footing. I've landed on my backside many a time while training horses this trick.

Did You Know?

In principle, every trick has its own command so that the horse can better differentiate between them. "Hold" is a universally applicable cue that can be used for many exercises. You should always use this voice command when the horse should take something in his mouth and not let go.

Cleaning Up

Once your horse has gradually developed an interest in the tricks that ask him to take something in his mouth, you can provide endless variations. I can give you one more suggestion: *Cleaning Up* is another very popular trick. With this one, you'll definitely get any audience to smile—and your fellow boarders to envy you!

TOUCH IT

Position three or four cones in a row on the ground. It's a good idea to rub the rim of the first cone with an apple, making it more palatable to the horse to take the object in his mouth. Or, perhaps he's already getting so familiar with trick training that this is no longer necessary.

Point toward the cone, give your voice command (for example, "Hold"), and praise your horse as soon as he picks up the cone.

Cones come in various materials; some are made of hard plastic, which makes them lighter. There are big and small models. Try different varieties to see which type your horse prefers putting in his mouth.

HOLD IT

In order for Romeo to have a better "grip" on the cone, I kick it over with my foot so that he can grasp the bottom edge. Some horses might prefer to bite the point of the upper edge and lift it up that way.

If you and your horse had fun with the cones, practice a bit more! Aim to have your horse not only take the cone in his mouth but also lift it up and hand it to you.

A GOOD HELPER

Point again to the cone, give the voice command for your horse to pick it up, then take the cone away immediately with your hand—before the horse lets it drop. Praise him again. Your horse will quickly learn that he gets praised, and perhaps a treat, when he picks things up and hands them over to you.

In this way, you can cultivate a "helper," and the horse will first be given a big treat after he's "cleaned up" the third or fourth cone.

Playing Soccer

After all these tricks, you may wish to end with a little action. Does your horse enjoy "playing ball"? If your horse likes to nuzzle, push, and kick a large, horse-safe ball when given a hand signal and voice command, you can take the next step and practice *Playing Soccer* with him. Start by trying this trick on the ground, then move on to Play Soccer under saddle.

FEEL FOR THE BALL

Give your horse the same voice command that you use on the ground, for example, "Kick." Follow the ball, guiding your horse directly toward it, on a long rein. At first, he'll often just "kick" it accidentally. Begin at the walk, but once that's going well, you can try building in a little trot. It's best to do so when the ball is far away, so the horse can trot a few strides before he gets to it.

SCORE A GOAL

To make the soccer game more interesting, position two barrels or cones to mark a goal in your riding arena. Try to get the ball through the goal. You'll find it's not really that easy. You must ride precisely in order to push the ball in the desired direction. If your horse evades your aids, you will miss your shot.

TEAMS

If there are others at your barn who would like to Play Soccer, you can also have a real soccer game with two or four players. When you're playing with two horse-and-rider teams, the first team to get the ball through the goal wins. You can also add a second goal, which evens out the game and prevents it from becoming too wild. Remember to stay gentle with your aids, even in the midst of serious competition!

DESENSITIZATION

Remember to be aware and be careful: In the course of the soccer game, the ball can roll under the horse's belly or hit his legs from behind. As mentioned, you should first practice from the ground, with the horse wearing a halter and lead rope, in order to get him used to the rolling ball. Move the ball away from your horse and toward him. He should be 100 percent comfortable with this before you try playing a soccer game with friends.

Wellness Program

When you've practiced your tricks diligently, make sure your horse has the wonderful closure to the work that he has earned. Enjoy how fun it was to work together. Give your horse a reward, such as a massage with a rubber curry comb or a relaxing circling of the tail (a TTouch technique taught by Linda Tellington-Jones in her book *The Ultimate Horse Behavior and Training Book*). Maybe you want to bring the day to a close with a trail ride or by turning your horse out to pasture. What does your horse enjoy most? What does he especially like? Incorporate that into your completed training session.

ENJOYMENT

Shir Khan enjoys rolling when his work is finished—he twists and turns like a cat. You can see how it does him good! Romeo also loves throwing himself on the sand after a training session. Most of the time, he stays there and lounges lazily on the ground for a bit. But, it's not because he's totally exhausted—we enjoy practicing together, but I always end the training session before the horse is tired and loses his concentration.

FULL SPEED AHEAD

Finally, there's always the best reward for any horse: Turnout in the pasture! There, his horse buddies may already be waiting for a group run through the field, a little mutual grooming, then eating some tasty grass in peace and quiet...or taking a nap.

This way, the horse ends his day satisfied and relaxed. And you both can look forward to a great day of practice again tomorrow!

MOTIVATED

When things are going really well, it's time to end your training session. If you end on a good note with your horse, you'll find he'll be motivated to cooperate with you on the next day of training. Perhaps through trick training, you'll discover a totally new side to your horse. You will certainly improve your understanding and connection.

Introducing the Artists

I believe that by looking at the photos in this book, you can recognize that not only we riders but also our horses have a lot of fun practicing the different tricks I described. The work brings us together and lets us playfully work on many skills, including finding new ways to solve problems. We all wish you and your horse the same kind of enjoyment and success with trick training!

ANDREA AND FRISKY

Andrea has ridden since early childhood, and as a youth she attended major competitions. She regularly rides my horse Romeo to help his training progress. Three years ago, Andrea and her family discovered the American Miniature Horse. Since then, breeding Minis has become her passion.

ANKE AND DUKE

Anke started out trail riding on her neighbor's horses. After some time at a riding academy, she became a team with her sometimes very strong-willed Haflinger, Duke. They've been together for six years. Through groundwork and trick training, the two have developed a wonderful connection.

PETRA AND LUNA

Petra owns four horses, including a
Shetland Pony and an Andalusian mare.
For many years, she's given instruction on
both trick training and classical
groundwork. Iberian horses are her
passion. Petra has helped with the training
of my horses, especially in the trick
training department.

JENNIFER AND ROMI

Jenny is the youngest "artist" in this book.
She and Romi have been a team for seven
years and they simply work together—no
matter if they're competing at a dressage
show, jumping, trail riding, riding with a
neck ring only, or practicing tricks. The two
stick together through thick and thin.

ACKNOWLEDGMENTS

I want to thank all who took part in the photo sessions for this book, including those in the background, such as Horst Streitferdt, Sandra Reitenback, and Birgit Bohnet. I also want to acknowledge all the helpers who were present over the course of the many days it took to capture what we needed in pictures—many thanks for your help and support!

Index

Page numbers in *italics* indicate illustrations.